Christmas

Meli — with lot

love from Daddy &

Mum.

X X

CW01433501

Perth
in old picture postcards

Norman Watson

European Library   ZALTBOMMEL/THE NETHERLANDS

Cover picture:

Perth Museum seen in a locally-produced postcard of 1908. In 1822, as a mark of respect to local magistrate Thomas Hay Marshall, a number of subscribers combined to erect a monument in his memory – a building which would also serve to contain halls for the public library and a 'museum for the reception of natural curiosities, antiquities and works of art'. In this card there is a glimpse of the tenements of Bridge Lane and Castle Wynd, wich were demolished to make way for the proposed art gallery in 1920.

The author:

Norman Watson was born, brought up and lives in Perth. He is a journalist with the Dundee Courier, for which he writes news and current affairs features. His own publications include 'Dundee's Suffragettes' (1990) and 'Perth in Postcards' (1991). He is the proprietor of the Kinnoull Hill Tearoom in Perth. An honours graduate, he is currently completing an external PhD research degree in political science with the Open University.

Acknowledgements:

Grateful thanks to Shirley E. Blair and Linda McGill for their expert assistance in the preparation of the text.

Postcards from the author's collection.

BACK IN TIME

GB ISBN 90 288 5758 3
© 1993 European Library – Zaltbommel/The Netherlands
Second edition, 2001: reprint of the original edition of 1993.

European Library
post office box 49
NL – 5300 AA Zaltbommel/The Netherlands
telephone: 0031 418 513144
fax: 0031 418 515515
e-mail: publisher@eurobib.nl

INTRODUCTION

For a city so rich in history, Perth has few surviving historical buildings. Yet, for 20 golden years at the turn of the century, pioneering photographers recorded the life and times of the city on picture postcards.

Yet, this legacy is merely a timewarp in a proud history which spans not 20 years, but 2,000.

Most of Perth's early records have long been lost, destroyed or plundered, leaving historians only to wonder at the extent of the settlement's early size and influence. In his discussion on the early medieval history of Perth, set out in the transactions of the Perthshire Society of Natural Science (1974), Professor A.A.M. Duncan suggests that a flourishing community existed in the High Street and Watergate during the early part of the 12th century.

Perth certainly prospered. By the middle of the 12th century, the town's revenue yield – income mostly from customs on goods passing through its harbour – was more than any other Scottish burgh's. By the year 1180, the town boasted two principal gates, High Street port and South Street port. It had a perimeter wall, a castle and a mighty kirk. By then, streets such as the Watergate, Kirkgate, Speygate and Skinnergate were probably established.

It is worth dwelling on this early period, for Perth retained much of its medieval, walled shape until the construction of its Georgian suburbs around 1800. Between times, it became a royal burgh, Scotland's ancient capital and her seat of government. Kings were crowned at nearby Scone and made their home in Perth. On its Inches – peerless gems – witches were burned and feuds settled. Its great river opened up trade with the four corners of the globe and spawned the town's great fishing and dyeing traditions.

But Perth could not live in the past. Guided by civic visionaries, such as Lord Provost Thomas Hay Marshall, the town began to shake off its medieval appearance in the 18th century. Under his guidance, the North Inch doubled in size and a new bridge was proposed. The old council chambers, a new post-office and the first of many new streets were planned.

The Scottish enlightenment, however, projected Perth in other directions, notably in business and commerce. And, by the mid-19th century, the foundations for Perth's future prosperity were laid when its key industries of dyeing, whisky blending and insurance were founded. A well-worn tale surrounds the contemporary founders of Perth's two biggest-selling whiskies, Dewar's and Bell's. Finding themselves too early for a church meeting, John Dewar and Arthur Bell decided to have a little refreshment. 'What will you have?' asked Bell. 'A Bell's,' replied Dewar. 'It would not do to go into the meeting smelling of whisky.'

Fine public buildings were created in this century of stunning achievement – the new academy in 1804, the sheriff court in 1819, the museum in 1822, the county infirmary in 1836 and the magnificent Bank of Scotland office in St. John Street in 1848. Later came impressive ecclesiastical buildings, including St. Matthew's Church (1871) and St. Leonard's in the Fields (1885).

The 20th century brought Edwardian elegance, but it also led to important social change. Two kings were crowned. Motor cars arrived. Aeroplanes took off. The Irish rebelled, as did women. National Insurance was adopted, the Titanic sunk and, of course, the Great War affected every home in the country.

These events were captured for posterity by Britain's leading postcard publishers. Cards were a cheap and cheery novelty which, almost overnight, allowed the great majority of the adult population to communicate a few words in writing.

As the nation changed, so Perth changed. While the reign of Queen Victoria had added splendour in the shape of impressive buildings, the priority in the new century was to expand the city's boundaries. Soon the new suburbs of Letham, Muirton and Moncriefe were under construction.

They paved the way for developments at Hillyland, Burghmuir, North Muirton and, latterly, the Western Edge. None, however, compromised the city's wonderful setting. Nestling amid a glittering panorama of mountains, Perth has retained its unique character and charm, while working hard to maximise its popularity. Its annual arts festival, agricultural show and highland games attract thousands of visitors. First class leisure facilities, such as the swimming and leisure complex, the indoor ice and bowling rinks, McDiarmid Park football stadium and the Gannochy sports arena, form a sporting jigsaw unmatched in Scotland. In recent years, Perth has been voted the best district in Britain in which to live, best twin town in Britain and winner of the best town category in the Britain in Bloom competition.

These are events which, 90 years ago, would have been certain to feature on commemorative postcards. Not now. Cards today remain the preserve of the tourist. Curiously, the most popular scenes among modern postcards are remarkably similar to those published 90 years ago – Kinnoull Hill, the Fair Maid's House, Perth Bridge and St. John's Kirk.

In some ways, time DOES stand still.

Athol Place and Rose Terrace, North Inch. Perth. E 31422

1. The expansion of Perth's medieval boundaries and the creation of its Georgian 'new town' towards the end of the 19th century, led to the construction of elegant new streets such as Atholl Place and Rose Terrace. Note the iron railings around the perimeter of the North Inch in this postcard of 1913. They were subsequently removed to aid the war effort.

High Street.   Perth.

2. This view of Perth High Street, near the theatre, was taken in 1903, the year in which the Scone and Perth Omnibus Company, launched in 1894, became Perth Corporation Tramways. Coincidentally, the Perth-bound and Scone-bound horse-drawn trams pass each other in this scene. As the horse era drew to a close, with the coming of electricity to the tramways in 1905, temporary stables were erected at Bridgend, at a site still known by some as 'Cuddies' Grave'.

HIGH STREET, PERTH.

3. The 'electric cars' were launched in Perth on 31st October 1905 and were instantly popular. Some 25,000 passengers were carried in their first month of operation. An ornate and impressive Victorian lamp standard appears in the foreground. Wouldn't it look well with a modern-day hanging basket?

4. Remaining in the High Street, we now see the theatre area with more evidence of costume outside than in! Doubtless down-town promenading was as popular then as now!

High Street, Perth.

5. Buses arrived in Perth in the inter-war years, signalling the end of the tram in 1929. In another view of the High Street, the Craigie bus uplifts passengers outside the old post office building, now demolished. Just as time – and progress – has taken us from horse-drawn to electric trams, and then to motor buses, so too can we see how Perth High Street has developed from two-way traffic in this scene, to one-way in the 1960s, to pedestrianisation today.

6. The sparse cottages which existed in Barnhill mushroomed into a small community when the new Perth to Dundee turnpike road was opened in 1829. Although it has recently lost its post office and shop, Barnhill retains its character and its links with the past. A few metres beyond this turn-of-the-century view the old toll house remains, complete with its archaic table of charges.

7. The foundation stone for Smeaton's Bridge was laid by the Earl of Kinnoull in October 1776, ending a span of 150 years when faith in bridges had 'dried up' because of flood damage, and townsfolk had relied on ferries to ply across the Tay. Perth Bridge, as it is more commonly known, was opened to the public five years later in October 1781, at a total cost of £26,631.

"North British Railway Series."

Tay St.
M.W.&Co.,E.

Perth

8. This official North British Railway souvenir postcard of 1904 looks from the railway bridge towards Tay Street. Prominent in the centre are the distinctive Doric pillars of Perth's sheriff court, built in Greek Revival style in 1819-1820. Sheep graze peacefully on Moncrieffe Island in the foreground!

East Bridge Street, Perth

9. At first glance, little seems to have changed since this 1906 view, looking towards East Bridge Street. In actuality, a transformation has occurred. The corner shop has gone, as has the tenement opposite and Potterhill House behind it. There is neither shoe shop nor carpet store now and few bowler hats or women in ankle-length skirts. And not many horses!

10. The work of the distinguished Victorian architect Sir Robert Reid, the academy buildings in Rose Terrace were opened in 1807, following a generous gift of land by Lord Provost Thomas Hay Marshall. The clock and statue of Britania were added in 1886. Perth Academy moved to its present home at Viewlands in 1932. The Junior School is on parade in this postcard of 1907.

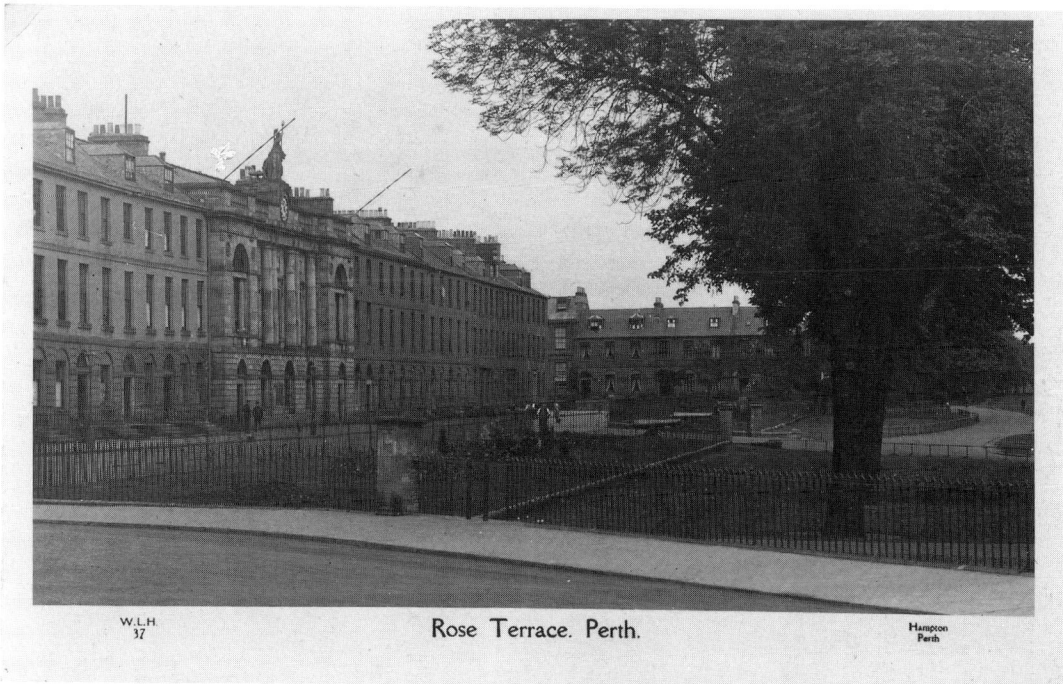

W.L.H.
37

Rose Terrace. Perth.

Hampton
Perth

11. The North Inch, opposite Rose Terrace, retains to this day an old wash pole from the days when townswomen used Perth's ancient public parks for washing and bleaching. It was common then to see groups of women engaged around a pot with a fire beneath it, before laying out clothes in allotted, pegged-out areas. In the 19th century the town council provided a night watchman to look after the clothes – a custom which passed when the communal wash house opened in Mill Street.

Avenue, North Inch, Perth. 597.

12. Unlike a similar structure in Dundee which has recently benefited from restoration, Perth's Victorian bandstand came to an unhappy end in 1958 when it was demolished and sold for scrap. Erected in 1891, the cost of £312 being borne by a member of the Pullar family of dyers, the bandstand became one of Perth's most popular meeting places. It also fulfilled civic functions. From there, in 1947, the Queen Mother accepted the freedom of the city on behalf of the Black Watch.

Atholl Street, Perth.

13. As the town's boundaries spread north and south and Perth's Georgian 'new town' took shape Atholl Street, seen here in 1905, became an important and elegant thoroughfare linking Smeaton's Bridge with the new North road, which had replaced the old Highland road across the North Inch. At Atholl Street's junction with Kinnoull Street stood the Theatre Royal, opened in 1820.

THE FLOOD, NORTH INCH AND PERTH BRIDGE.

14. Perth was hit by serious flooding in January 1903, an event captured on camera by the city's fledgling postcard photographers. As the Dundee Courier of 2nd February put it, the North Inch floodwater extended 'from the bandstand to the Albert Monument'. The artistic 'floating' of this card makes it unclear whether the dog in the foreground is walking, swimming – or sinking!

SIR ROBERT PULLAR L.L.D. M.P.
PERTH. 1907.

15. From humble beginnings in two small rooms in 1824 Robert Pullar and a group of six assistants began the dyeing and cleaning business, which, at one time, saw 16,000 curtains repaired each week, 40,000 pairs of gloves 'rehabilitated' every month, and which boasted the largest drycleaning machine in the world, capable of cleaning carpets measuring 100 yards square.

16. Perth station, not so long ago, had all sorts of platform entertainments, but few as popular as Campbell's confectionery kiosk. This card, from around 1920, displays sweets at 2½d a quarter. How times have changed! The enamel signs advertising Fry's Chocolate are now collectors' items.

PERTH STATION   MAIN SOUTH-GOING PLATFORM.

17. Perth station's main southgoing platform, seen in this postcard of 1918, was established to complement the opening of the rail link between Perth and London on 15th May 1848. The large clock in the background exists to this day and is the work of the Edinburgh firm John Ritchie & Son.

THE OLD SCONE BUS & DRIVER JAMIE.

18. A horse-drawn tram service began in Perth in 1895. They were superseded by electric cars in 1905 (accompanied by a price rise of $^1/_2$d to 1d) and permitted to increase their speed to 12 mph. This card bears the caption 'The old Scone bus & driver Jamie'.

19. Smile for the camera! This fascinating portrait of a Perth family firm dates from the 1890s and shows the premises of J. Banks and Son at 128 High Street. Prominent in the window are bales of string and hemp.

CHERRYBANK

20. This rare postcard of a Perth suburb shows Cherrybank in 1906, then – as now – a prosperous residential district on the city's western edge. Cherrybank, in fact, was previously a small hamlet on the lands of Pitheavlis, by-passed by the old Stirling road, which travelled up Needless Road and Necessity Brae. The need to increase the city's housing base in the early part of this century, combined with the location of the western tramway terminus, brought rapid expansion.

Carr's Croft, Craigie, Perth.   J.K.T. FAIR CITY Series.
                                                  P.

21. As Perth's housing modernised in the late 19th century, the remaining pockets of inferior slum dwellings were pulled down. One of the last thatched rows was Carr's Croft in the Craigie district. As this 1904 postcard indicates, conditions for residents must have been extremely harsh.

South Methven Street, Perth

654

22. In medieval times, Methven Street ran parallel to the town's lade and formed Perth's western boundary. It took its name, presumably, from a route to Methven, then one of the principal communities close to the city. This real photo postcard from around 1920 shows South Methven Street as a hive of commercial activity. Note the overhead electrical tramway lines.

23. This early study of Methven Street demonstrates the allure of the camera around the turn of the century. Most likely the work of a local photographer, it is unsigned and therefore difficult to attribute. The buildings on the left have since made way for the award-winning Clydesdale Bank/McCash & Hunter complex.

24. Andrew Laing & Co.'s grocery store, on the corner of South Street and St. John Street, is clearly decorated for a great occasion: the royal visit of 1914. Prominent among nearby flags and bunting, and confronting their majesties on the royal route, was a large banner demanding an end to the forcible feeding of suffragette prisoners at Perth jail!

25. The King and Queen's visit to Perth, to open the new infirmary in 1914, is recorded on several locally-produced postcards. This example shows Queen Mary leading the royal party to plant a ceremonial tree. Over 1,000 guests in specially-constructed stands watched the ceremony.

South Inch Avenue, Perth.

RELIABLE WH SERIES.

26. The famous avenue of elms on the South Inch culminated in one of Perth's finest buildings, the Round House, formerly the city's waterworks. It was built in 1832 after a design by Dr. Adam Anderson, rector of Perth Academy. Several schemes to supply clean water to Perth were considered. Dr. Anderson's solution was to pump water from a well on Moncrieffe Island into his new building, for storage in the dome. It was used until 1965.

MARSHALL PLACE, PERTH. 48

27. Postcards can also help to show that some streets in Perth have changed comparatively little over passing years. For example, Marshall Place, seen here in 1905, bears much resemblance to today's scene. The days without double yellow lines and endless bed-and-breakfast signs have a certain attraction, though!

ONE OF PERTHS OLD WORTHIES,
DOCTOR DAVID TODD.

28. Dr. David Todd, one of Perth's Edwardian worthies, had a habit of writing to Queen Victoria and printing pamphlets on his dreams. His epitaph in Wellshill Cemetery reads: 'Eccentric Dr. Todd; Here lies beneath the sod; His fitful chequered life; With wants and woes was rife; But here he sleeps in peace; His wants and woes have ceased; The elm tree's branches shade; His last and lowly bed.'

29. 'The keen frost still prevails and for more than a week the Tay has been completely frost bound.' So said the Perthshire Courier in February 1895, after the river at Perth became ice-bound to a depth of several feet. Stories abound of hundreds of people taking to the ice – to play cricket and curling and even to roast an ox!

Red Cross Hospital, PERTH.

30. Built as the County and City Infirmary and eventually housing fever victims, war wounded and T.B. sufferers, this imposing façade in County Place is now to take on a new lease of life as the headquarters of Perth libraries. Opened in 1836-1837, at a cost of £6,000, it lost its status as an infirmary in 1914 when Perth Royal was opened. It subsequently became the headquarters of Perth County Council.

31. As a war-time Red Cross and V.A.D. hospital, many servicemen must have passed through the County Place infirmary without a hitch. Not so with this poor lad!

32. In May 1910 King Edward VII died, leaving the then Prince of Wales to succeed to the British throne as King George V. Tradition in Perth, as in other towns, dictated that the public proclamation of the new King was made at the town cross – in Perth's case, at the junction of the Skinnergate and High Street.

33. Another much-admired building to change hands in recent years is the former General Accident headquarters at the east end of the High Street. Opened in 1901 as the prestigious new home of the Perth-based insurance giants, it has latterly housed Perth & Kinross District Council. It is seen here decorated for the 1911 coronation.

Perth Coronation Procession, 1911.
Pageant passing through South Street Port Arch.

34. A spectacular coronation procession took place in Perth on 22nd June 1911 to mark the crowning of King George V. A crowd, estimated at 20,000 and held back by mounted policemen, followed the bands, choirs, performers and decorated floats on the parade's route between the Inches. Here, the procession passes beneath a specially-constructed floral arch at South Street port.

35. The 1911 procession provides us with some of our best local postcards. Here we see the car – or float – of Britannia arriving at the North Inch. King Neptune, on the 'ship's' prow, appears to be taking the weight off his feet. Veterans of the Indian and Crimean wars featured prominently in the parade.

36. A Dundee-Perth rail service began on 22nd May 1847. Until a wooden railbridge was constructed two years later, trains terminated at Barnhill on the east side of the river and passengers crossed to Perth by ferry boat. This bridge was subsequently replaced by the present structure in 1862, which is seen here being crossed by an early locomotive of the Scottish Central Railway.

Prince's Street, Perth.

37. This card dates from around 1925, towards the end of the Golden Age of postcards, and shows Prince's Street, looking northwards towards St. John's Kirk. On the left is the Prince's Street sub-post office, now closed. Postcard production fell into decline after the First World War and street scenes showing motor cars are rather scarcer than those depicting tram cars.

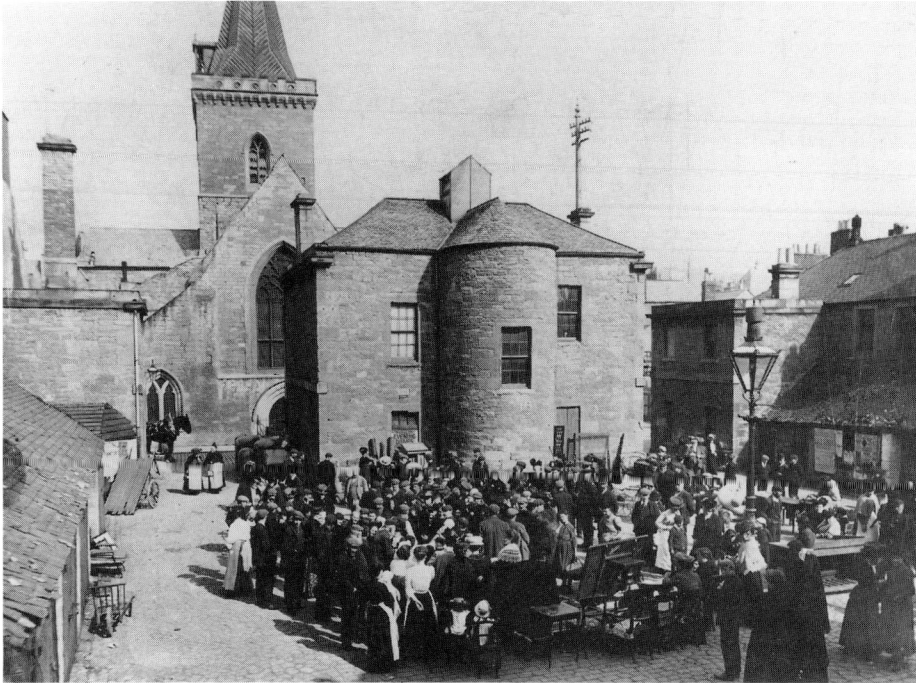

38. The old city hall is seen here, about 1910, with one of the final open-air auctions or 'roups' underway ... fittingly on the site of Perth's medieval commercial centre or Flesh Market. Built in 1845, the old hall seated over 1,500 people in its prime. Alas, it was in a dilapidated state by the time this picture was taken.

New City Hall, Perth. Opened by Lord Dunedin, 29th. April 1911.

39. Perth's new city hall was opened by Lord Dunedin in 1911, after a competition for its design. Constructed of Angus sandstone, it has become famous – or infamous! – in recent years for hosting political conferences. The new hall had seating for 2,100 people. Its cost of £30,000 was met by Perth Corporation.

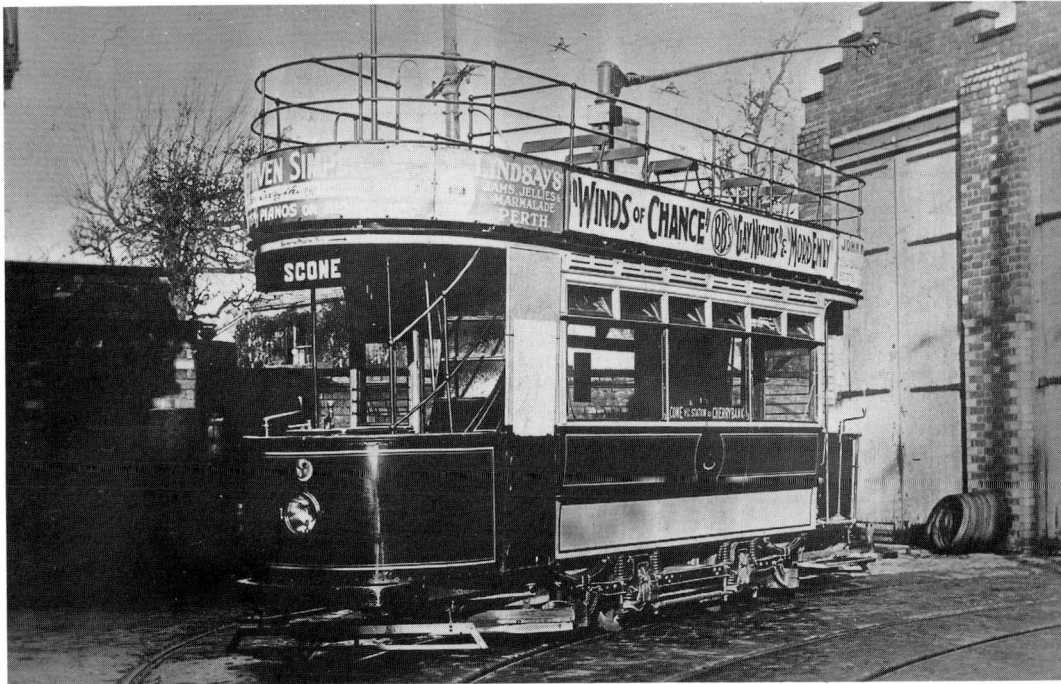

40. This fine postcard shows the Scone-Cherrybank tram No. 9 in all its glory at Scone depot. Perth's electric trams were among the smallest in the country. They ran on single tracks, with passing loops at intervals. The last tram in Perth ran on 19th January 1929.

41. Robert Henderson & Sons, of 226-228 High Street, were established in Perth for almost a century when, happily for us, this exquisite postcard was issued. Henderson's specialised in a line of goods which could easily roll off the tongues of their hard-pressed salesmen: 'Fish, game, poultry, fruit, flowers and plants.'

Fair Maids House, Perth

42. Although immortalised in a medieval setting by Sir Walter Scott in his Fair Maid of Perth, the present 'Fair Maid's House', which draws many an admiring glance from history-seeking visitors, actually dates from the end of the 19th century. Nearby, at Blackfriars, is the site of the Dominican monastery, founded by King Alexander II in 1231.

ST. JOHN'S PARISH CHURCH, PERTH. (EXTERIOR.)   98614.J.V.

43. Gifted by the monks of Dunfermline in the 12th century, St. John's, the parish church of Perth, has had a volatile, fascinating and well-documented history. Its undoubted highlight was John Knox's sermon from within its walls in 1559, which led to mob riots and the destruction of the town's finest buildings.

Gowrie House, Perth, (built 1520, taken down 1807)
noted for historical event called "The Gowrie Conspiracy" of 5th Aug. 1600.

01976

J. K. T. P. FAIR CITY SERIES.

44. Gowrie House was once one of Perth's finest and most historic buildings. Built in 1520, it was home to the powerful Ruthven family. It fell into disrepute in 1600 after an alleged attempt on the life of King James VI failed. But whether the conspiracy was an effort on the part of the Ruthvens to get rid of the King, or on the part of the King to get rid of the Ruthvens, is in doubt. It is a jest of time that the present court house occupies the position, where Gowrie House once stood!

Infirmary and York Place, Perth

45. Making haste, to avoid the on-coming Cherrybank-bound tram in York Place, is a well-stacked hand cart. Carts and barrows appear frequently in early postcards and must have been extremely popular, and probably indispensable, in Perth at the turn of the century.

SCONE CAMP MILITARY SPORTS Sep 1R /16

46. From 1893, temporary post offices functioned at a number of summer camps used by volunteer forces for annual manoeuvres. A camp was established in the grounds of Scone Palace and welcomed its first troops, the Gordon Highlanders, in 1915.

Opening of the New Golf Course, Perth

47. They're all set to tee off at the opening of Perth's new golf course at Craigie – but the Fair City's love affair with the game goes back much further. According to kirk records of 1604, a miscreant called Robertson had to sit in the seat of repentance for 'playing at the gowf on the Sabbath on the North Inch at the time of preaching'.

1038   ROYAL INFIRMARY, PERTH, FROM SOUTH WEST

48. The Royal Infirmary, on lands at Tullylumb, was opened amid much ceremony by the King and Queen in 1914. Royalty recently returned to the infirmary when, in August 1993, its major annexe was declared opened by the Princess Royal. This card, postmarked July 1914, was one of a set of eight published to mark the opening.

Northern. District School, Perth.

684

49. Northern District School, lying between Dunkeld Road and Balhousie Street, was one of the city's largest public buildings when this photograph was taken. This view is one of the earliest recorded postcards produced by Wood's of Perth. It is marked number 16 in their purchase ledger and is taken from a glass negative, bought from a local photographer on 21st September 1903.

50. An unusual Perth postcard, captioned 'Jock, the Unpaid Policeman'. One would assume it refers to the goose standing to attention and, no doubt, on alert, by the side of one of Perth's more recognisable constables.

51. Pullar's fire station was situated between Union Lane and Foundry Lane at 16 Kinnoull Street. The brigade first appears documented in 1859, making it Perth's first dedicated fire brigade. The horse-drawn pump in the postcard is possibly the Shand Mason double vertical steam engine, used at Pullar's in the early 1900s.

IN AFFECTIONATE REMEMBRANCE OF

RING OUT THE OLD RING IN THE NEW

THEY DID THEIR WORK THEIR DAY IS DONE

THE PERTH HORSE CARS

WHICH SUCCUMBED TO AN ELECTRIC SHOCK ON TUESDAY OCTOBER 31st 1905

52. The use of a black border to signify the 'passing away' of horse-drawn tram cars was a tool utilised by several Edwardian postcard pioneers. This example, by local publisher John K. Taylor, is a fitting tribute. The 'People's Journal' of 17th February 1905 reported that 'in four weeks up to January 17, drawings from the Perth tramways amount to £685 18s 2d and that the number of passengers totalled 143,721'.

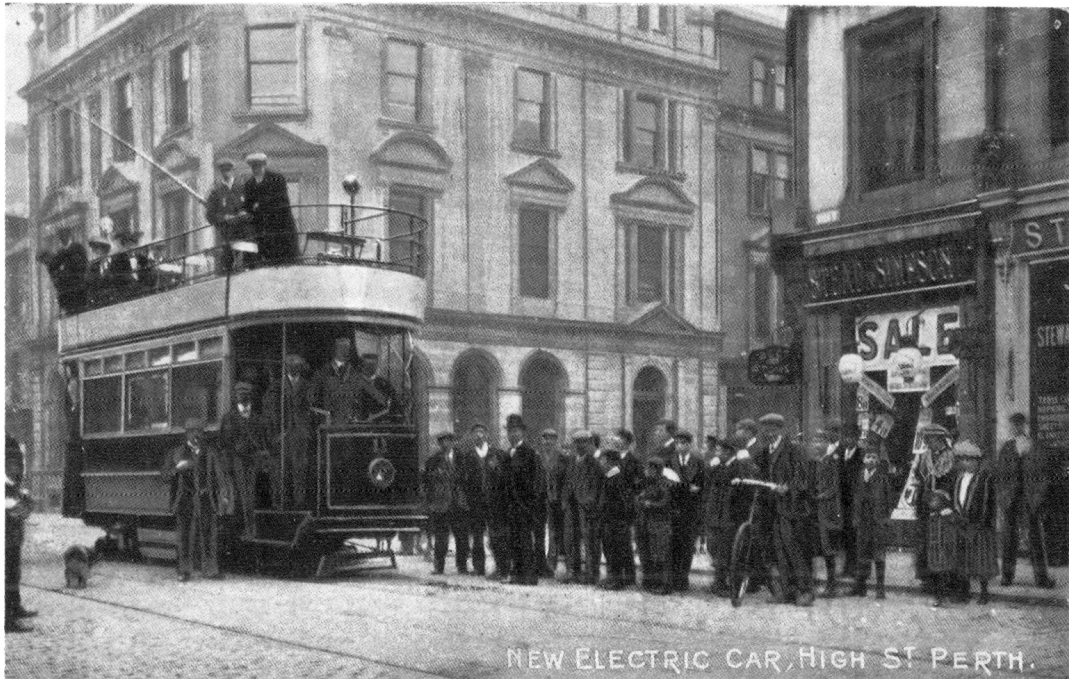

53. The inauguration of electric tram cars in Perth in 1905 was, by all accounts, a splendid event. The public turned out in thousands to see the new vehicles and, by evening, with a car decorated with 360 electric lights and with the Corporation Band generating music from the upper deck, the whole affair took on a carnival mood. This commemorative postcard reflects the great interest in the new machines.

5048.

THE KINNOULL TOWER, KINNOULL HILL, PERTH.

54. This famous tower, for 200 years a focal point for visitors to Kinnoull Hill, is no more than a folly. It was built in the 18th century by the Earl of Kinnoull after he had viewed similar structures above the Rhine in Germany. Steel bands were placed around the tower in 1970, when it was deemed in danger of collapse. 'We climbed this last Sunday and you get a grand view,' writes the sender of this card.

THE "SEE SAW," BUCKIE BRAES, PERTH.

55. If you didn't take your sweetheart to Kinnoull Hill, chances are you would have headed for Buckie Braes, the perfect alternative! This charming, wooded playground, on the lower slopes of Necessity Brae, has remained popular to this day. Wood's of Perth alone published around 20 postcards of this beauty spot between 1904 and 1918.

56. This somewhat ragged postcard from 1911 shows a lovely scene: a special day out to Perth for children from the Lanarkshire village of Eastfield, courtesy of North British Railways. Although the children's finery is difficult to see in this picture, it is of a quality only surpassed by that on the locomotive itself.

FLOOD AT PERTH STATION. 8-7-16.

57. An unusual postcard, showing a flood in Perth station in July, 1916. The 'People's Journal' said of the inundation: 'In its relentless fury, the great river swept all before it. For the first time in the memory of the oldest inhabitants, the permanent way of the Caledonian Railway was covered with water. Many people watched the novel spectacle of trains churning water into a turbulent loch.'

BLACK WATCH INSPECTION, PERTH BARRACKS.

58. Built in 1792 as cavalry barracks and formerly the home of the Perth Militia, the extensive barracks at the top of Atholl Street dominated life in Perth for decades, not least when marauding Black Watch squaddies spent their leave – and pay – in the city's hostelries. The barracks were demolished in various stages to make way for the new police station, the inner ring road and a sheltered housing complex.

CORSIEHILL PERTH Nº 62

59. The thatched cottage seen in this 1904 postcard of Corsiehill is now a tearoom. Formerly, it was the 'hall' in the tiny hamlet, where ladies gathered for embroidery and evening ceilidhs were held. Corsiehill itself is an ancient smuggling community, nestling conveniently on the old drove road to Kinfauns and the Carse of Gowrie.

60. All seems peaceful and calm as pedestrians stroll across Perth Bridge in this postcard from 1913. Yet at one time they would have had to pay for the privilege. Until the end of the 19th century it was a toll bridge, with a charge of one farthing to cross. The tram seen on the left is a direct ancestor of the Scone-Cherrybank bus route.

61. When Perth prison opened in 1842, it housed 328 prisoners, including 109 women. The building had been erected originally in 1811, and was opened the following year for prisoners from the Napoleonic wars. It closed a year later and remained empty until it was re-opened as the country's first General Service Prison.

INNER COURTYARD OF H.M. GENERAL PRISON, PERTH. It covers an area of 14 acres, and consists of a centre block, with four wings or blocks—Hospital, Bakehouse, Washing-house, &c. The Tower was used for the supervision of French prisoners.

Bonspiel at Hillyland Pond, Perthshire.

62. This postcard, by Nicoll's of South Methven Street, dates from 1910 and shows a remarkable bonspiel involving hundreds of curlers at Hillyland pond. The Pullar's factory in the background once used 40,000 gallons of cleaning fluid every day.

63. The old ice rink in Dunkeld Road recently made way for a busy fast-food operation. In its heyday, however, the rink was home to Perth Panthers ice hockey team, to generations of free skaters and was the scene of Chuck Hay's memorable 'home win' in the curling world championships.

No. 10   BARNHILL FROM ST. JOHN'S TOWER   J. E. C. PERTH

64. This unusual postcard by local publisher James Craven of North Methven Street shows Barnhill from St. John's tower. The card dates from 1919, at a time when the wooded slopes of Kinnoull Hill were, clearly, sparsely populated. The Victoria Bridge, now demolished, is seen on the left.

65. Although trams operated in Perth from 1895, there was no tramway in Craigie until April 1898 when a horse-drawn service began, travelling via King Street, St. Leonard's Bank and Priory Place, the Craigie Street seen in this local postcard of 1906. Railings, cobbles, gas lamps and trams have long disappeared.

THE BINN TOWER AND VALLEY OF THE TAY, PERTH. 5098.

66. How stark and menacing the Binn tower looks, devoid of the tree cover which shrouds it today! Both the Binn and Kinnoull towers have much in common, as both were 18th-century follies. Having said that, there's life in the old place yet ... well, very nearly. In 1992, Perth & Kinross District Council received a planning application to turn the ruined tower into a home.

BLUE CAUM KATE, One of Perth's Old Worthies.

What do you think of her?

67. 'What do you think of her?' reads the legend on the front of a 1905 card, showing Perth worthie Blue Caum Kate. Kate took her name from the bars of pungent blue soap she peddled on Perth's streets. She lived in a house in Canal Street, now demolished. Despite her appearance, it is said she was well spoken and not in any way coarse.

68. This 1914 postcard depicts the Perthshire Half Holiday inter-county football team. Interestingly, the photograph was taken at the recreation ground, first home of St. Johnstone. Postcards of St. Johnstone are comparatively rare and no local card showing a match in progress is believed to exist from this period.

69. This rare card shows woodsmen gathered at Corsiehill on the eastern edge of the city in 1917. Trees on Kinnoull Hill were felled at this time to aid the war effort and this temporary sawmill was established on the flat ground at Corsiehill, adjacent to the quarry.

70. The 'Fechney', off the Glasgow road, was the popular name for the Fechney industrial school. There, young boys were taught practical skills – on the way, hopefully, to being reformed. What was left of this once-impressive building was demolished recently to make way for housing.

71. This delightful postcard shows the boys and bandmaster of the Fechney industrial school band. Although undated, it is possible that the boys were smartly dressed and displaying a powerful ensemble of instruments for the coronation procession of 1911.

THE KINFAUNS CASTLE ON THE TAY. 671

72. Taking a trip down the Tay on a paddle steamer was a popular pursuit at the turn of the century. This local postcard of 1906 shows the S.S. Kinfauns Castle, appropriately passing the hamlet of that name.

A VIEW FROM THE TERRACE OF THE ROYAL GEORGE HOTEL, PERTH.

73. Precious little has changed in the exterior of the Royal George Hotel in the 60-odd years since this picture was taken. Today, the George retains much of the air of tranquillity and charm which this peaceful scene portrays. And, of course, it still enjoys the same splendid outlook over the river!

74. Displaying the coat of arms of Perth, bordered by Royal Stewart tartan and showing a scene of the city from the south, this card is a wonderful example of the art of the Edwardian postcard publisher.

SCOTLAND'S BEAUTY SPOTS

PERTH FROM BRIDGEND

75. The Golden Age of the picture postcard dated from around 1902 to 1918. During that time, millions were sent and avidly collected. It is a legacy which has inspired a multitude of modern-day collectors, many of whom live in what this delightful card calls 'Scotland's Beauty Spot' – the city of Perth.

76. Finally, the author's grandmother appears, second left, on a card postmarked 1910. The women are seen on the old family farm at Cramflat, near Luncarty. The intriguing message on the reverse reads: 'Arrived home safe. Found chickens all alive.'